# Rotary Devotion

POETS OUT LOUD

Elisabeth Frost, *series editor*

# Rotary Devotion

## Gary Keenan

Fordham University Press   New York   2017

Fordham University Press has no responsibility for the persistence
or accuracy of URLs for external or third-party Internet websites
referred to in this publication and does not guarantee that
any content on such websites is, or will remain, accurate or
appropriate.

Fordham University Press also publishes its books in a variety of
electronic formats. Some content that appears in print may not be
available in electronic books.

Visit us online at www.fordhampress.com.

Library of Congress Control Number: 2017941386.

Printed in the United States of America

19 18 17    5 4 3 2 1

First edition

# Foreword

*by Alice Fulton*

Gary Keenan's collection is the sort that—like the truth—dazzles gradually. Its structural and substantive variety forestalls tedium: one can't predict the next move, and this quality of surprise is, for me, a necessary component of poetics. While Keenan is drawn to traditional lyric subjects—childhood, time, memory, mortality—he infuses them with a freshness that never seems strained. The book's title evokes its salient themes, such as communal rituals, the cyclical patterns of nature, the sacredness of the quotidian. Mindfulness shines through these ontological poems that mark—and sometimes celebrate—the nuanced complexity of ordinary experience.

The poems' structures are as engaging as their content. In addition to beautifully crafted free verse, there's a villanelle whose focus is perfectly suited to its form, and several subtly end-rhymed poems. "Improvisation on a Theft of Light" invents a fascinating nonce form that torques around short lines of repeated function words. Keenan's sense of the line is canny and well informed; his language is musical but never sounds as if it were composed by metronome; his excursions into genre are sometimes revisionary. There are odes that come to terms with limitation and disappointment, lyrics that take a gently sardonic stand toward American culture. The tonal range is nuanced and varied: tender, self-critical, reverent, sincere, or playful notes are sounded within the same poem, and heavier passages are leavened with flashes of humor. "Slow Storm"—a discursive poem that muses on chaos theory, Heraclitus, choice and chance—ends with a piece of disarming advice: "Face the wind and think of saxophones." "Portrait of the Ghost of a Flea" notes, "There are few gaps in conversation / That a large slice of key lime pie can't fill." The poems are wise without being tendentious, charming yet free of whimsy, poignant but never sentimental.

As this suggests, Gary Keenan is a poet capable of extreme seriousness and serious delightfulness. *Rotary Devotion*, his first collection, is deeply attentive to the rigors and joys of being alive, and it conveys this consciousness with sustained delicacy and profound wit.

# Contents

*I.*

Point of No Return   3

Materialist Fantasia   4

Dead Rooster   5

Sunlight in the Alleyway   6

Slow Storm   9

Emptiness   11

*II.*

Entropy: An Ode   15

Fence Factory   17

The Liberation of Melancholy   18

Accommodation Ode   20

Complicity   21

July 4, 1984   22

The Limits to Self-Observation   23

*III.*

The Rest of the Days of My First Life   27

Portrait of the Ghost of a Flea   30

Improvisation in a Time of Unemployment   31

Absolution   32

Alchemy Alley   33

Landscape with Stuff in the Way   35

*IV.*

Improvisation on a Theft of Light   39

Elegy on the Death of Mark Strand   41

Variable Rates of Change   42

A Common End   44

Just Between You and Me   45

The Light Takes Forever   46

Coda   48


Acknowledgments   51

# Rotary Devotion

*I.*

# Point of No Return

Before we get started, I'd like to point out
That there are too many books with titles
Like *Film as Film* and *Who Am I, Really*
For me to get excited about literature as a field.
I'm not the type to attract words like madcap
Or zany, but at breakfast, sorting through
All twelve grains of my granola for a unifying trope,
A feeling of giddy absence spilled from my spoon.
Today I'll walk with the muse, I thought.

I can see now it was too late,
I was already in the company of another kind of spring,
One in which laundry figured prominently.
Across the park, the squat brownstone library
Offered refuge from lilacs and hummingbirds,
Weathered benches crowded with guitarists.

Someone must have planned today, or at least requested
The salient features. Small children in overalls
Danced around a blanket full of food,
Dancing and spinning their limbs to transparency
Until their clothes seemed to hang on a line in the wind.

As they collapsed laughing, I resolved to tell you,
Hoping to find a way to reveal their whirling
Braids and hands, now that I speak of

Body as the lens between world and spirit.

# Materialist Fantasia

Remember when each day lodged in April,
A cobalt sky and clouds like fat grey fists
Coming at you? The work of being born
Lasts past trampled crocuses.
No importance announces itself:
Daffodils need no fanfare to be seen
As yellow bells stuck mid-ring in the garden.
That world of sleep, a muffled sonata of blood,
Is left behind but never abandoned.

French bread and black coffee in a hot bath.
Scatting to *Der Wunderbare Mandarin*
While ironing a shirt. Split red buds
Shine on sunlit trees outside the kitchen.
The cluttered house, all shingle and shutter
Made homey by a ravel of cats, wet clothes,
And appliances, is a precarious barricade,
Beyond which lies a home with no address.
This second dwelling, like a nomad's tent
Staked lightly on the ground, has little room
For ornament, being less building, more garment.

The natural world's a thing to knock apart,
Phrase by phrase, cell by cell, to recombine
In praise or panic. The starched shirt is worn,
The margarine spread thin, the flower fixed
To a lapel: each gesture advances the day,
Though singly their charm is weak.
Thrown together, they mesh and tear and stain
Until the sun becomes a kind of attire.
It's that moment, seeing the necessity
Of living two lives to know one, that stuns.
And the difficulty. Where to stand?
Where to let the light strike? Where to look?

# Dead Rooster

Each time I return, the barn's in ruins,
The truck in the forest settled to fenders,
Upholstery picked apart by birds for nests.
I reach the birch where my brother stumbled.
It still grows through the rusted wagon wheel
That bruised his skull. A few lady slippers
Poke though pine needles, and across the field
Finches flock, a gold cloud over red sumac.

I could wander all day
Where yards give way to woods
And old pastures fill up with pines.
Somehow it happens—I hear shotguns
In the morning distance, the noon chorus
Of frogs and woodpeckers, and voices of boys
Coming through the swamp. There I am,
Lying in tall grass like a wasp in amber,
Hoping the boys don't see me
And the hunters leave the ducks in the sky.

I know where the wild blackberries grow,
How to jump from rock to rock across the stream,
Which tree gives the best view of the houses.
Can I share my hands, can I tell why I love
How this pine tree blackens them as I climb,
Or explain the taste of treetop air?
The higher you go, the smaller things get—
My mother down there calling, she could fit
In my pocket. She stands beneath the oaks
Lining Scotland Street, hands on hips,
And watches me wave as I hurry down the limbs.

# Sunlight in the Alleyway

We have our reasons for staying put
                in the river of consequences,
                                if only for the moment
noon washes clean
                bricks caked with the soot
                                of a history no one notices
in pictures full of bustled silks,
                    trolleys horse-powered and the people
                                  all sepia and serious.

Every photo is a death
            foretold, an exit recalled, hubbub
                            hushed into pixels, arrested light.
The orphans kneeling in white nightgowns,
                hands folded in prayer, gone. Urchins
                        in patched britches sleeping on a stoop,
awakened to a more lasting dream
                none can tell. The blacksmith's clangor
                    scrapped with the last wood frame building
on the block. Everyone in hats,
            frozen in the film and flash.

                                  And this day like the last,
the next imperceptible wave
                of dust drifting through windows,
                        an afternoon full of other days
and ghostly neighbors seeing
            the same shadows of iron ladders
                        and stairs slanting toward earth
and heaven. In my poverty
            lies my treasure, that I have nothing
                    left but imagination and windows,

the songs that move me to sing,
                children dancing to my banjo,
                                perfect in their present joy.
So let this be a lens
                into your own timekeeping,
                                that regard you pay
to passersby, to the traces
                of a lost city that you, too,
                                will one day inhabit
with nothing but inaudible echoes
                of your own death song
                                dressing your bones,
the love you spoke loudest
                living longest. Take me with you
                                as one of those ghosts
shaped by another century
                of war and wonder, speaking
                                as your brother and witness
that we walked these streets
                together at times, as strangers
                                to ourselves but capable
of smiling at the world
                however silly that seemed.
                                Remember you will forget
most of this life, just as you
                will be forgotten in time,
                                my love, my heart and hands
given to you without
                price, with nothing
                                expected in return
except the hope that you
                also give away what
                                you value most to the least of those

you meet as you can.

        Now clouds mute

                the sun as predicted,

A scent of rain faint

          in the air cooling toward

                  the next hour.

Today, awaiting a downpour,

       I am happy among my books

             having coffee with my cats.

## Slow Storm

To start in pain and end in revelation,
Tree limbs scattered on wet streets
And parked cars. The path from one leaf
To the next is realized by stratagem
And impulse, best thought of as a corollary
To chaos theory rather than fate as such.
Months ago dragonflies collided in Brazil,
One of those unobserved exemptions
Insurers term "acts of God," and their spin,
A tiny frenzy of translucent wings, now whips
The North Atlantic into a deadly froth.
You can't ponder the same universe twice,
And it's a good thing—otherwise, watching
Tulips dry into paper flames
Or waking for sex at six a.m. would lose
Some grace. This deserves a hymn or two,
Even if no one is listening.

To take shelter is futile, but to speak
Of shelter offers real refuge.
You need all your strength choosing
A spot to watch waves tangle
With fog at the jetty's end,
And yet you don't see enough: the clouds
Are torn apart behind your back,
Sandbars piece themselves together underwater,
Attractive pairs, strings, clusters—
Abstract traces of order beyond the mind—
Revolve around a dead seal rolling in the surf.
The eyes are gone, the snout eaten away,
The mottled body a companion to thought.
Millennia of choice and accident end
With carbon compounds sinking in the sand,
The possibility of a fossil nearly nil.

Some days you feel more like a stone than a sponge,
Other times you doubt your own existence—
*Dubito ergo sum* is hardly a rallying cry,
But it will have to do. Then a casual acquaintance
Leaves a note on the kitchen table:
*Sharks are never bored.*
Everything changes, as if reading the sentence

Scarred your retina. Out there,
Beyond the continental shelf, beneath the swirl,
Killers work fresh variations
Of an old theme. You catch a glimmer of life
Without art and almost submit.
Rain in the grass saves you.
The wind kicks up carousels of sand
And straw, a mystery and mere data,
Something you will one day reinvent. Maybe tomorrow.
Face the wind and think of saxophones.

# Emptiness

Sometimes I hear my father's voice in mine
before I speak, a whiskey'd baritone.
A pause, the feeling passes, and I'm fine.

A family tree roots in the jagged mind
whose sleep instructs the body bone by bone.
Sometimes I hear my father's voice in mine

and wonder if I'm sliding past my prime
with neither sons nor daughters of my own.
A pause, the feeling passes, and I'm fine,

I really am, there's my piano, time
enough to plow through Proust, chat on the phone.
Sometimes I hear my father's voice in mine

when a caller asks if I'll subscribe to *Time*
and I warn him never again to call my home.
A pause, the feeling passes, and I'm fine,

return to writing while my heart unwinds
stray phrases playing off its metronome.
Sometimes I hear my father's voice in mine.
A pause, the feeling passes, and I'm fine.

*II.*

# Entropy: An Ode

Everything is incomplete, each day
revised past recognition. Penciled-out passages
beg close study, luring thoughts
hard to catch, harder to ignore—
the world is full of holes.
The mind adores a vacuum
crammed with constellations, comets,
probes launched toward hypothetical orbs
affirming the imagined quality of the universe.

Those open-eyed dawns bedded in dunes,
sipping coffee, feeding donuts to gulls,
never ended, they just belong
around other people. Someday someone
will recall waves we saw, all iridescent dazzle,
and experience the sea as blood,
bones so much coral, soul swimming
toward the moon's flimsy twin
winking just beyond the breakers.

And when the waters recede into canyons
carved through layered crust and we wake
beside a mesa, nothing but sage to guide us
to the horizon, what new raptures
seize the vulture's eye? A jackrabbit
scuffing the dust? Lightning fifty miles west?
Deer graze among aspen at dusk.
There is no limit to the beauty,
only ratios of lenses, mirrors, red clouds

rolling over hidden cities. Stars
so far off they nearly don't exist
offer all they can to our neighborhood,
and the technologies that posit their being

bring part of us to life as well,
these steaming streets and blunt buildings
dreamed by a deity sprawled
glassy-eyed in a gutter abyss, too wasted
to grab dimes of starlight scattered on tar.

# Fence Factory

In bed my ears still ring
From eight hammers, each swung
In a separate rhythm that yields
No clear order, only a sheet of thuds
As if drummers at a Moroccan wedding
Pounded silence into the hearts
Of witnesses. It is that quiet
On the shop floor, best recognized
When all eight heads strike wood at once
And the concussion startles men
New enough to catch the distinction.
Some naked wonder permeates the wood:
Pine pickets lean and cool, the musky odor
Of wet cedar. A drill bit bores through oak,
And smoke plumes sweet as the hashish
We do at dinner. All of us get high
Except Billy, who has worked
Piece rate so long that no machine
Can nail as fast and leave so clean a plank.
After eight years of hoisting a 24-ounce hammer,
His right forearm is toned like marble
And seems to lead his body through the shift.
It knows motion means money. As I lie
Trying to sleep with the taste of sawdust
And beer and bread in my throat,
Billy stands at a bench in his basement
Working overtime, his exquisite arm rising and falling
As he beats three-penny nails into silence.

# The Liberation of Melancholy

*for Laura and Neil*

In a windowless office, imagine a beach
so bright, waves rise green and roll,

the sun above a city piercing clouds
with accents, angles, edges keen to cut

a heart from its sack and toss the muscle
into the air like a ball or baby.

Take a letter. Any at all.
Don't tell a soul it's Q,

just invoke quiet as pulses quicken.
Our voices—reedy, rowdy as a hurdy-gurdy—

never stop, but doesn't that imply
they never started but simply define

that steady state through which bodies pass?
A blue candle flicks light across a planet,

a crystal bowl holds galaxies to grab.
Everything in line and fine.

Everything okay, no matter
what matter may be—we've gone through enough

shag and tact to puff our way past any blow.
*Semper infidelis,* the fallen angels say.

Relax in my arms, sleep if you like;
I'll wake you when the moon is loveliest.

The choices many, hours few:
We do what we can to each other,

forgive what we must. Every vehicle
runs through an engine, rusts at seams.

I'm no different, even if the fire
Feels alive as your skin, my lips cinders.

I've already taken from you words you won't miss
and admit I'm no wiser.

## Accommodation Ode

I rarely find myself empty under rafters,
Poking around dusty boxes for schoolboy
Souvenirs as autumn slowly loosens its grip
Leaf by leaf. I can still taste Styrofoam
And watery hot chocolate, hear the roar
Of neighbors and their penchant for instant nostalgia,
The football games that tortured their children
When it snowed most Novembers and ponds
Glistened with thick white ice by Christmas.

Thinking back, it amazes me anyone survived
The ignoble truth that life is mostly disappointment
After puberty in the suburbs. My best friend
Was my bike after all, a shiny white-walled Columbia
That could outrace all the Schwinns in Christendom,
At least that's what I imagined on my paper route.
Each dawn I rode with Charlemagne and Tencendur,
Tossing folded *Boston Globes* like so many battle-axes
At front doors that stood for Moors on my campaign.

I never went to war. I'm not afraid to die,
Though I'd miss reading, the wind in tall grass,
The babble of Spanish everywhere. Blessings
I never earned litter my path and if I paused for each,
I'd never get home to practice guitar. This is my life,
At least I think it is, and the solace of uncertainty
In the face of unavoidable pain makes me no more a monk
Than a mountebank. I'll probably never read all my books.
That's heaven enough in whatever hell I find.

# Complicity

I'm used to being watched, to having my measure
Of unearned success despite the energy I've spent

Running in place. The nominal pressures of thoughts
Bubbling in my tea kettle skull whistle brightly—

I shall know neither them nor their like without strain
Even as I pound the well-worn mitt of childhood

Into a more serviceable catch-all rationale.
I have trouble remembering being dwarfed

By bushes and snow drifts, afraid of adults
I needed most. Oh, to be a bird of prey

Soaring on updrafts and delighting in sight,
Or a sleek-muscled coil of claws and incisors

Sitting in pitiless grandeur atop the food-chain,
Instead of an habitué of chain restaurants,

Gnawing on the early-bird special. I've lost instincts
For prowling or scavenging or at the very least

Shopping with abandon. Now I simply listen as men
Say with great certainty that they are uncertain,

That the balm for my poverty is to make them richer,
That I should settle for less while they demand more.

I don't laugh, nor do I cry. I don't buy a gun or fashion
A bomb from household chemicals. I decide to vote

For whichever rich man might harm me less.

# July 4, 1984

The wet sand yields like the wall
Of a womb—pliant, enveloping each jog
With particular resistance. Sand dollars
And crab legs, the glittering dead cod,
Lie in line plotting the neap.
The sand's a fine spot for ends.
It conforms. Waves slip in it beating
Themselves to foam. A drag extends.

Gutted by gulls, a ray's white belly
Flashes in the sun. Wounds form eyes
And a jagged mouth about to holler
Last words before the face subsides
Beneath the surf. The prime duty
Is to dig one's own abyss, to seek the bones
The face hides. Decay brings a final beauty.
Brine whittles a fit for the prominent stone.

A ratty blanket, fragrant oils,
A fresh batch of shells to display—
Each lingers in the day's eventual
Plan as a signal of place. A biplane
Sputters past towing a sentence:
*Celebrate Independence At BayBank's 24 Hr. Teller.*
The shadows slide up the beach like serpents
Emerging from weedy swells.

# The Limits to Self-Observation

*Can a picture contain a full and precise picture of itself?*
*. . . On a finite canvass this is impossible, except in the trivial*
*case that the picture is the picture of itself. (Then the picture*
*is also the picture of the picture of itself, and the picture of the*
*picture of the picture of itself). —Thomas Breuer, "Limits to*
*Self-Observation"*

You find a spot you think begins your end
and sit and watch the sunlight stab through clouds;

the red-wing blackbird's flashing epaulets
illuminate the rushes where it flits

attacking sparrows. You're hung-over, sore
and bruised from pounding on the doors

of perception: no one's home. The mansion
in a moment will be chalk, the world mere tons

of excrement and offal. Still, the coffee's
warm. Art and work can wait. A single bee

flies slowly, flower to flower, in the cool air,
and in the guitar's buzzing strings you hear

laments of Appalachia and Roscommon,
the blues of Willie Brown and Charlie Patton,

the truths your throat cannot emit except
in tones unlovely, hoarse, nasal, bereft

of any music but your own; and yet you sing
before you speak to anyone. Nothing

in your stomach but caffeine and bagel.
No thought in your mind. Feet on the table.

A blade of sunlight bisecting the garden,
a few faint insects hovering, wings applauding

mornings spent in idleness and rapture
that won't be framed, repeated, painted, captured.

*III.*

# The Rest of the Days of My First Life

How might one intuit waking life while asleep? Often I dream
  of having
Already risen into the morning air, fully dressed but for my
  trousers,
Fueled with caffeine and corn muffin and outrage at the day's
  headlines

And bound for battle with the bulls of rippling lethargy, a
  toreador of torpor,
Only to wake in warm silk sheets, a beautiful but married
  woman in my arms
And cat claws combing through my eyebrows. O, that the days
  were so green,

The sun's blue pallor might be visible to all! That's why I keep a
  spare star
In my wallet, to illuminate codes scribbled in lemon juice along
  the margins
Of each day's reportage. A UPS truck idles, full of destinations
  and discoveries,

Driver more heroic for the advertising, the muscular angel of a
  cargo cult
With its unfortunate fecal colors and acronym puns. I'll never
  sign
For a neighbor's parcel again. I may not even accept my own.
  I've enough crosses

And naughts to cover every corner of this burg, my mayoral
  hopes be damned!
So foraging with one eye to the grindstone has exacted a
  cyclopean price
I'm unable to pay except via my arts and what subterfuges they
  betoken in kind.

Today's editorial is smeared on my cuffs, and someone keeps
   poking me from behind
With what feels like a young goat's new-sprouted horn but must
   surely be an umbrella
Though the sky is clear of everything but airplanes, contrails,
   and winds made visible

By scraps of newsprint spinning down the sidewalk with the rest
   of us. I've read enough
To know the stories inscribed therein are mere chapters in the
   autobiography of a dream,
And pity the dreamer who wakes before the denouement. Still,
   the pricks of ambition

Will not rouse me from my hobbyhorse. I enjoy anticipating the
   reservations of guests
When presented with motley bonbons, without a hint of which
   holds the cherry,
Which the stone. The hand posed in divine indecision, the
   absolute uncertainty

Over unintended consequences—my moments of intense faith,
   if you will. I can praise
A random universe generating one me per eternity, as well as the
   next *poète maudit.*
I still sing that looping hymn the refrigerator taught me in my
   youth, the cycle

Of human desires for a cool drink in the afternoon when the
   house pulses
With machinery and napping hearts, the transubstantiation of
   jello, the tabernacle
For butter. If sopranissimo is no longer within range, so be it.
   Pianissimo must serve.

And yet the thrill of listening intently also becomes a quality of
   attention

For attention's sake alone, and by this sign one might find the
    exit and leave
Secure in all that comes next, immune to confusion by the
    embrace of same.

# Portrait of the Ghost of a Flea

I've lately come to the realization of my dreams
And have nothing left for sleep but this sweaty duvet
And a salami and muenster on rye. I don't even like salami.
I'm used to noodles; I've grown fond of fronds
Waving green above waves of blue and white,
Yet my portfolio is held in trust. Where does that leave me?
In a cab with nothing smaller than a hundred?
On an empty Amtrak platform 3 A.M.?
My best friend told me a story once about an elephant
Running amok in a market, and I wish I could recall
The punch line, but I have a subconscious fear
Of comedy that makes me appear ridiculous
At even the most idiotic occasions. I went
To several specialists and baffled them.
That was worth the expense, believe me.
There are few gaps in conversation
That a large slice of key lime pie can't fill,
And the sheer wonder of such moments irrigates
The encroaching stupor with light and melody,
With songs of thanksgiving for potholders,
For indoor plumbing, any old thing made new.
Under that sort of pressure, I tumble now and then
Yet manage to land on the ground, grateful
For gravity once more, that such a weak force
Arranges heavenly bodies to the eye's delight—
How many summer nights have I spent
In no one's arms but these, rapt
And humming with unspoken urge!
So don't expect the world when you open the envelope.
That way, the little planet that falls into your palm
Will tickle like a wet kiss placed lightly there.

# Improvisation in a Time of Unemployment

I've been working on brewing the perfect cup of coffee with little luck
and jitters that would jettison a less substantial soul from its coffin

and this is my curse today that was my blessing yesterday,
to be so full of myself that even the beasties in my gut protest

in voices to rival those of the muses for my ears: I've come
to believe in all those tongues singing their secrets to me alone

more so than any declared purpose or plastic-coated card
pinned to my lapel offering a greeting I'd never actually utter;

their language is as direct as disease, infective, communicable,
incurable except by ordeal—I think of the soul

as nature's most implausible blossom, the supreme beauty
and consolation in an otherwise unsympathetic chaos;

some take sugar to sweeten the kick of bitter beans,
but not me: nothing competes with the bitterness

of my own making or the pleasures of steeping in blood,
keeping my chalk outline moving through another day

in the Empire of Unchecked Appetites, fasting while others gorge
and feasting on their sad corpulence as if a diet of worms

were something to enjoy and not merely be.

# Absolution

I know you are out there
Hiding from what you've done
Just as the man you built hid
After realizing his nakedness
Was at odds with your own.

It must be hard to know
What you'll do when the sun,
Your spare, glorious dynamo,
Shrinks to massive char
Consuming worlds spun

Of the same stuff, less radiant
But equal in your eye. This ornate
Calculus will creak to a halt,
Leave you alone at last
Without measure, still, celibate.

So make the most of us.
We are still naked, still awed
By the nakedness you conceal.

# Alchemy Alley

## I.

Inscriptions of sunlight on brick,
Italic echoes of each arch, and morning air
Warping above heat vents surround the mirror
Of coffee in a glass cup and the time
It takes to pull apart small bread.
This is the body of solitude,
Day chilling before noon. Thin faces
Held in many panes of glass become
Masks for the lumpen skull, the skin
An accident of steady feeding.

## II.

The legless man lies with the queen
Of plastic bags. They polish and barter terms
Suffered beyond their precise doorway
To shape a lexicon for the climate
Piled about them. She recalls the path
Of the parade after the killing paused,
How brass gave day a rival light
And sorrow stopped the wail of saxophones.
Hot dust clogged silk braids, epaulets
And music without melody, only endless cadenzas.

## III.

Paracelsus, did you conceive your science
As a wheel on which to throw
The wet clay of the mind? Or was it
Something other than knowledge
Of bodies, some act of coding a lust

Between magnet and metal? That tiny universe
Inside you, a void littered with light, cooled.
Through flint and iron, sulfur and saltpeter,
Lead's heart remained still, refined
By failure. Dull things have their own aplomb.

IV.

Thus water, as earth's blood, must move
To index desire, the hunger of circling vultures.
The world beneath words, utterly crucial,
Proves in its purity a marvel and refuge,
Bonding with sexual purpose each person
To the project of making the invisible
Visible. This task, so familiar to trees,
Is for language-bearers a method
Of irrigation, and the sun,
Their great reservoir of love.

V.

One need not be ashamed to walk alone
Straight into the woods' mottled clatter
Singing lightly for the day.
Beyond the rotted footbridge, wet moss
And stagnant water shine on the path home,
A greater forest in each branch and leaf.
In the city, a keystone's vocation
Of absorbing stress for a wall's sake
Is blessed only by the mason's craft.
Whole lives depend on such work.

# Landscape with Stuff in the Way

*It is an artificial world* —Wallace Stevens

When the frame is more beautiful than the picture,
Look at the frame. That small piece of advice
Never looked bigger than it did a moment ago,
When only it separated me from the chaos
That was my seedbed and will be my grave.
Ah, the sleep of suburbia, moth wings scraping
The window screen across from the night-light,
The leathery flutter of bats above the willows—
Night still comes over me like a symphony
From a far FM broadcast, moon conducting
Crickets in the tall grass, choir of stars
Waiting for the grace note that cues their fall.
I used to lie awake for hours, afraid of missing something.
How new desire seemed then!—every cell
Itched to tell its own story to charm a beloved
Who never quite appeared as the dream dissolved,
More sister than mother, but stranger to both.

Why did adults always have things to say?
Did they practice in advance, or just make it up?
I'd ponder such issues from the dark end of the hallway,
While my parents entertained neighbors with clinking highballs
And Nelson Riddle strings. I grew up surrounded
By genius—it glowed in robin hatchlings, hissed
Through red oak leaves in a summer storm
Like violas behind Nat King Cole's breathy tenor—
Though no one thought to point this out to me.
I thank the silence in these matters, the immanent
Inadequacy of talk. My friends were idiots, mostly,
Marionette adults with cigarettes and stolen beers
And drunk with inherited hate for Jews,
Blacks, each other, themselves—not even
Their own pets were safe—pity the turtle

Or hamster kept in those bedrooms.

I claimed the silence, or it claimed me.
It was sanctuary during my trials of prosperity
When I was encouraged to dream the right dreams
Of a property owner, to dress as if fear were my business
And business boomed. I learned to lie, said I wanted
A house, pool, and neighbors like me, or said
Nothing and let the big bellies have their little chuckles
While I caddied them toward the clubhouse.
I did nothing to earn my escape. Nothing worked just fine.
It still does. When in doubt, doubt—a finer mantra
Was never mumbled. I love the strangeness of my life,
The awkward moments when I think I don't know
Myself at all—am I a farmer or rancher?—and then
Catch myself thinking about who I apparently am not,
And whether those two might get along in a future life
If not this one. This past Memorial Day, I went
Back to the land of lawn furniture for a family cookout,
And spent most of the day with my nieces and nephews
Teaching them to play rock and roll loud enough
To silence their parents. The kids played a tiny synth,
Wastebasket drums with wooden spoons, a junk guitar,
Recorder and marbles-in-tupperware maracas,
And I picked mandolin. We sang a Hank Williams song
About the fate of all ramblers and wrote one together
On the I-IV-V chords in a thoroughly unoriginal way
That had kept me in my body throughout childhood
And still does. I felt this was the baddest influence
I could offer the next generation of my genetic pool,
To give a bunch of six- and seven-year-olds
The key to a really dangerous code that, if handled right,
Would wreck every expectation parents and grandparents had,
That something holy might arise in imagination
And claim their childish bodies for its own.

*IV.*

# Improvisation on a Theft of Light

*for Amy Sue Rosen*

The conditions of various bodies are the condition of one body,
One mind the thoughts of many minds

As if, as if,

You are lying in your bed, head stitched,
And I am the tumor the doctors removed,

Only, only

I have already embraced your bones and organs
With my multiform affections, and you have nothing

But, but

Your recollected arts, the pellucid jars of fluids,
The doors that leap open for gigantic babies,

And, and,

In the moments when flocks of rabbis plummet
From the ceiling and dance the mystery

Of, of

Their beards, the ecstasy is as palpable as anything
We might leave in each other, a child, a kiss,

Or, or

The simple awareness that our paths
Continually cross and tangle daily, nightly,

For, for

Each body carries that which the others cannot bear,
So we might know a love beyond our capability,

When, when

All we have left is an echo of our thought
Fading into the luminous, the sought, sought.

# Elegy on the Death of Mark Strand

There is an island in my eye no one has visited
But many have seen, mistaking it for the mountain
Atop which the Buddha sits with goats and vultures,
Singing the last song the mind admits before oblivion.
I'm told the song knows no measure, that wind
Carries the tune by day, and water, by night,
Hence the Buddha sits by a stream so that not one note
Escapes the ears of those who need music most.

But I was not born to speak of mountains, of islands,
As if my tongue were a lexicon of departures
For terra incognita, my lips a map of farewell kisses,
As pleasant as that would have been. This life
Filled me with breaths I never pretended to own
Though I paid attention to each, curious
As to how inhalation changed to exhortation
And who might be behind the beating wings
That quickened with recognitions that only made me
More beautiful in the dark when no one could tell
Who was talking. Now one of us goes silent,

Another pipes up with grieving sigh; you lean
Into the sound as if it were intended for you alone
In a language you've never dared share until now.
The words themselves were never enough,
Always indicating something more to be felt,
Leaving the silence in their wake more strange,
More yours, more mine. So I keep this scrap of blood
In my wallet to remind me, whenever I doubt
My capacity to disappear into grammar,
That I follow your nimble climb into unknowing,
The sky cloudless in sorrow, the stars
Chanting your name into someone else.

# Variable Rates of Change

*for Bek Andoloro*

As the avenues fill with afternoon light
So, too, do my hands become acquainted

With the volume of your radiant presence
While you occupy rooms that barely fit

The life your mind demands of your body.
Cartographers of lust may claim that dawn

And dusk are but borders, customhouses
Wherein light inspects dark, and night, the day,

But I would prowl those zones alone
If that meant a purer light for you, a deeper sleep.

I do not matter, and what I have, I give
To the furnace and compost heap.

These bones are mere wicker,
This skin the antimacassar of a mind

Worn thin with indecision. I cannot
Be followed for more than a day

Without collapsing beneath the bluster
Of it all, the rage to say, "It is thus," and then

The urge to deny even this. Once written,
My thoughts construct minds of their own,

And no doctoring will make me whole again.
I think of you often, or shall I say, we do so

With a gentle regard learned in your care,
That this compassion might operate

In the world, and with it, and through it.
Such thought never ceases, so long

As hymns are carved into clouds
And rained into gutters.

No one listens to me without wondering
If I am all here, for good cause—

I've never been more present nor more removed
From the ideas we hold of one another,

And in my middle age I've grown
Fond of the view closer to ground.

The silver haze of December lingers
By the parking meters. By the time I think,

"Can I use this?" I've been used.

# A Common End

Steaming buildings in the solstice night,
Tarpaulins snapping against the façade
Of condominiums, and the rattle
Raccoons make returning from their forays,
Are consecrated by a darker eye:
There is a field in which the white-tailed deer
Stands camouflaged, and one in which it dies.

Lemon tea brews, and a chaotic fog
Vents from the pot, traces of orange peel
And rosehips condensing on the windows.
It's snowing. Eddies of a higher wind
Curl around the chimneys and dormers,
The faint green cones of streetlight. The rooftop
A monotint of folded shadows.

The teapot drops. A thin red pool of tea
Spreads across the white floor. The shaken man
Sees himself kneeling beside it, watching
The tint shift as the accident expands.
It becomes a part of the self he keeps
Against winter, a roseate event
Cooling on linoleum.

# Just Between You and Me

A span of thirty years or two inches
Admits more starlight than either of us
Collects alone, and if a mole
Truly holds plans for the whole organism,
Ratios governing muons
Factors in the strings of galaxy clusters,
Then where we started matters less
Than staying together for a time
As missives arrive from outliers
About shopping malls as new ground for struggle,
Fish missing from the city aquarium,
A mock stroganoff recipe made with Rice Krispies
Sent by an Aunt Trixie neither one of us recalls:
We track these random reports wondering
If we need index cards or a mainframe,
And if the burgeoning database represents the world (you)
Or convenient lies about the world (me) or escape
From responsibility and revolution (that's it!),
Still we revolve around each other like twin suns,
Responding to the slightest wink or yawn,
Dreaming in tandem, telling tales over donuts
And dinner about events between meals,
Comparing your fear of falling off curbs
To my aversion to elevators, and though you suffer
Loss of feeling in your limbs you don't straggle
But lead me to that leap defining
Sexual ecstasy's absolute severance
Of the self, this body's spirit
Blooming on a withering stem,
This life a blindfold walk along cliffs,
Sea below thrashing in an uneasy marriage
To land: hear how they need each other,
How one wears the other down until they rest
Promontory against inlet, facing night
And darker skies as one.

# The Light Takes Forever

I'm frying butterfish and potatoes,
Watching collard greens wilt in the steamer,
And thinking about sunsets in Central Square.
I've worked there five years, enough time
To memorize the liquor stores
And thrift shops, the odors of curry
And coriander drifting out warm doorways.
Clusters of kids in untied Adidas
Stare at passersby and at each other:
A woman shifts her baby and shopping bags
Arm to arm: a madman kicks a pigeon
Outside a pizzeria. The subway
Arrives and leaves, sidewalk shaking
As if the earth sensed the growing chill
Of a January afternoon. Each day
I walk through such a scene, always new
Always composed of familiar elements,
And I struggle to see it as unique,
Feeling each step, each heartbeat as a choice.
Inside the fogged windows of a Burger King
Teenagers and their squirming children
Share dinner: if they were simply ugly,
If they would blend with the Styrofoam
And red and yellow packaging,
I would not have to praise them now,
But they are always beautiful, no matter
How much they begin to resemble the meal
Of grease and starch and sugar before them.
Their beauty is not based on pleasure
But persistence, a quality I admire most
When it appears unconscious. If my neighbors
See their lives as part of a longer life,
And each of them feels, as they glance at the sun

Going down behind the police station,
That the silken wash of red and blue sky
Is a prayer for union with that life,
What do they make of me, walking past
In my black boots and overcoat, black briefcase
Swinging by my side? I know this day
Of mine won't last. All the love and fine words
I try may not make winter less difficult.
Slowly, I learn to love the work, the rites
One makes of necessities, of meals.
Cooking relaxes me. I'm glad to know
I have an offering, an act performed with care.
Turning the fish. Setting two places. It's almost ready.

# Coda

I'm covering the creases of my palms
With clay gloves. If you insist we touch

They'll fissure, so let's simply salute
A common narcissism and proceed

With the destruction of this hour's dance,
Fixing the limits of intent and loss

With eyes cast left and hands that signify
Eclipse. Yesterday I watered sunlight

Instead of the Swedish ivy. Why not,
I thought, no one's looking. But sharing this,

I begin to blame you, so eagerly
Confirming my fear of human nature

With a nod, a co-conspirator's smile.
The mind construes the skin about the eyes

As semaphores fluttering when we sleep.
I know—I watched you sleep last night

And counted out the code to all your dreams.
Not much to report, the cipher's safe.

But more than once your hand moved up your leg,
Peripheral fears demanding you shield

Your focus. So much wisdom, such thin arms!
Yes, I could dress with lots more *savoir faire*.

And our correspondence, its insistent manner,
Inflames my desire for less wholesome terms.

I leave them to you. Measure your feelings
Against those relics: "hot jazz," "sachertorte,"

"flux." We both thought every word worth saying
Would cohere until there was between us

A third being, the sum of all we felt.

# Acknowledgments

"Slow Storm" appeared in *Georgia Review,* Fall 1993

"Emptiness" appeared in *In Posse Review, no.* 7, 1999

"Fence Factory" appeared in *Smokestack,* 1991

"The Liberation of Melancholy" appeared in the Winter 2016 issue of the *Moth Magazine*

"July 4, 1984" appeared in *Ploughshares* 13, no. 2, 1987

"The Limits to Self-Observation" appeared in *Exquisite Corpse,* no. 7, 2000

"The Rest of the Days of My First Life" appeared in *Courtland Review,* no. 26, Spring 2004

"Portrait of the Ghost of a Flea" appeared in *In Posse Review,* no. 7, 1999

"Rotary Devotion" appeared in *Exquisite Corpse,* no. 7, 2000

"Alchemy Alley" appeared in *Southern Poetry Review,* Summer 1996

"Landscape with Stuff in the Way" appeared in *Courtland Review,* no. 26, Spring 2004

"Improvisation on a Theft of Light" appeared in *Movement Research Performance Journal,* no. 22, 2001

"Variable Rates of Change" appeared in *Exquisite Corpse,* no. 7, 2000

"A Common End" appeared in *Brookyn Review,* no. 8, 1991

"The Light Takes Forever" appeared in *Appearances,* no. 23, 1995

"Just Between You and Me" appeared in *Appearances,* no. 27, 2001

"Coda" appeared in *oblék,* no. 12, 1993

POETS OUT LOUD
*Prize Winners*

Gary Keenan
*Rotary Devotion*

Michael D. Snediker
*The New York Editions*

Gregory Mahrer
*A Provisional Map of the Lost Continent*

Nancy K. Pearson
*The Whole by Contemplation of a Single Bone*

Daneen Wardrop
*Cyclorama*

Terrence Chiusano
*On Generation & Corruption*

Sara Michas-Martin
*Gray Matter*

Peter Streckfus
*Errings*

Amy Sara Carroll

*Fannie + Freddie: The Sentimentality of Post–9/11 Pornography*


Nicolas Hundley

*The Revolver in the Hive*


Julie Choffel

*The Hello Delay*


Michelle Naka Pierce

*Continuous Frieze Bordering Red*


Leslie C. Chang

*Things That No Longer Delight Me*


Amy Catanzano

*Multiversal*


Darcie Dennigan

*Corinna A-Maying the Apocalypse*


Karin Gottshall

*Crocus*


Jean Gallagher

*This Minute*

Lee Robinson

*Hearsay*


Janet Kaplan

*The Glazier's Country*


Robert Thomas

*Door to Door*


Julie Sheehan

*Thaw*


Jennifer Clarvoe

*Invisible Tender*